Who Takes Care of The Caregiver While They Care For Someone Who Has A Mental Health Illness

Renita Adira

Copyright © 2022 by Renita Adira

All Rights Reserved

WHO TAKES CARE OF THE CAREGIVER WHILE THEY CARE FOR SOMEONE WHO HAS A MENTAL HEALTH ILLNESS

Published by PREMIUM PUBLICATIONS

PO Box 891
Crown Point, IN 46308
www.premiumpublications.org

Printed in the United States of America

This workbook or parts thereof may not be used or reproduced in any form, stored in a retrieval system, or transmitted in any form by any means electronic, mechanical, photocopy, recording or otherwise without prior written permission of the publisher, except as provided by United States of America copyright law.

First Edition

Cover Design & Layout by Createbook.org

Library of Congress Control Number: 2022921523

ISBN: 978-0-9977451-3-9

This workbook is dedicated to the many people who cares for someone who has a mental health illness. I would like for you to know that you are not alone. I know that it feels like you are the only one who carries the weight of it all, but I promise you that there are others who can identify with what you are going through. I would like to encourage you to take the necessary steps towards making and keeping yourself healthy. Please remember that we can't make or force others to want to help themselves, we can only support and assist them along their journey. Caregivers are oftentimes neglected, rather they neglect themselves or other people neglect them; many caregivers end up on a road called out of gas. I would like to encourage you to first care for yourself, then second others. Don't allow people to decide how you are supposed to love yourself, care for yourself or how you should live life. Always make your own mental health a priority because you will be a greater benefit to others when you are at your best and healthiest.

When caring for someone who has a mental health illness you should always make sure that you are taking care of yourself first. It can be mentally draining to care for someone who has a mental health illness. Stop allowing the behavior of your love one to steal your peace or joy. No one knows all of what you may be going through but it is my prayer that you practice better self-care. My hopes are that you practice a greater level of mental wellness for yourself first. Be encouraged, live in your today and remember to take one day at a time.

The worries, problems and troubles of tomorrow will only keep you in bondage living with constant stress. Don't hurt yourself to help someone else, no matter who it is. It takes the willingness of all parties involved to bring about change. You are just as important as the person that you care for.

Contents

Introduction	vii
Ask yourself	x
1. A Letter to My Current Self	1
2. How did I Get Here	4
3. The Journey to becoming a Healthier whole you	8
4. It's About Me Too	13
5. The Mask of the Caregiver	16
6. Managing your Time	19
7. The Importance of Self-Care	23
8. Communicating Your Needs	26
9. Mental Clarity	29
10. Building a Support Team	32
11. Scheduling Time for Yourself	35
12. Daily Affirmation	38
13. A Letter to my Future Self	40

Introduction

Mental Health is screaming louder than ever. Mental Health is on the rise and more and more people are living with a mental health illness. From young to old it doesn't have a particular face or age. One of the hardest things in life for any parent or person, is to stand by and watch someone you love suffer in silence; knowing that you can't do anything to help them get better. The things that you do, or the efforts that you make to help them, only serves as a short-term fix. More people are assisting, caring, or supporting someone today then in times past. Rather it is someone who has a Mental Health illness, Cancer, HIV, AIDS, Autism, ADHD, Dementia, or an Alcohol or Substance addiction. The need to care for someone has grown and is steadily growing.

One of the saddest and most painful things about mental health, is there isn't enough awareness, help, support, or funding to help the many people who are in crises. Many caregivers start off strong but as time passes on, they too become just as weak and fragile as the person in whom they are caring for. The caregiver gives and gives and gives and gives, until he or she has nothing left for themselves or anyone else. Mental Health is not only hard for the person who has it. It is also hard for the caregiver. The caregiver gives in so many ways, rather it be words of encouragement, self-esteem building, or providing mental or emotional care. Oftentimes their efforts go unnoticed, and their pain gets ignored along with their own personal health.

If you can relate to anything that I have said thus far, please know that you are not alone. I know that you feel like you are, however; I want you to know that you are not. The reason why I wrote this book is to bring some level of comfort to the caregiver by letting you know that you are absolutely not alone. I hear your cries because those are the tears that I cry too. I can identify with your pain and your hurt because that's what I feel as well. I can also relate to your fears and anxiety because they are mines too. I even understand your anger and at times your bitterness. Let's walk this journey together so that you can began to heal and gain the mental clarity and emotional support that you need.

Even the strong needs support. Allow me to share some words of encouragement with you of what healthy caregivers looks like. You can't care for others in a healthy manner unless you first care for yourself. If you are not well and healthy first, how effective do you think you will be in caring for others? The strength of a healthy caregiver isn't about how much you can put out by depleting yourself. The truth of the matter is healthy caregiving is, how balanced you are while caring for others. Depletion is never an option when caring for others, no matter who it is. The healthy way to care for your own personal needs is to always do a self-check, stay balanced and regularly do an emotional, mental, physical, and spiritual check-in on yourself.

Allow this workbook to show you how to take your superman or superwoman cape off. This workbook will teach you why you can't be everything to everybody or everything to your love one. You are one person with the capacity that can only hold so much and endurance so much. Allow this workbook to put you on a journey to a healthier whole you. Mental Health is something that no one ask for, however; it has become a silent killer in our homes, schools, communities, place of work, and amongst the people in whom we care for and love.

Caregivers needs support just as much as the people in whom they are caring for. Don't allow who you are caring for to steal your joy or peace. Get the support that you need. Love yourself enough to care for your own needs in the following areas, mentally, emotionally, physically, and spiritually. It's time to work on you. I know it may feel like you are giving up on the person or people in whom you are caring for, but that is not the case. The truth is you are now deciding to now make you a priority. You are going to learn to care from a place of balance; so that you can support and assist and care for others in a healthier manner without forgetting that you also matter. You are just as important as the person or the peoples in whom you are caring for.

Ask yourself

What is your definition of being a Caregiver?
_____

Do you believe that you currently care for your love one in a healthy way?
_____

Who cares for you when you need to be cared for?
_____

What do you need?
_____

On a scale of – 1-5, 5 being the highest, how tired are you?
_____
_____
_____
_____
_____

A Letter to My Current Self

In this section you will write a letter to yourself that describes your current state of being where you are now. This letter should express how you feel, your current stress level, if you have a support system, etc. You will need to be really honest with yourself. Be truthful even if it hurts because you need to see where you are in your current state before completing the workbook. Take the mask off!

_____

_____

_____

_____

_____

_____

_____

_____

_____

_____

_____

_____

_____

_____

How did I Get Here

The question that many caregivers ask is how did I get here? Some know, while others don't have a clue. Many caregivers have made unhealthy practices of caregiving a part of their daily routine of life. Meanwhile others are on a quest seeking their how did they get here. Most caregivers have gotten lost in the act of caring and giving to the point their how doesn't matter anymore. Many caregivers find themselves just doing and feeling totally overwhelmed.

You shouldn't just do and do and give and give and think that is healthy for you. Also, you shouldn't keep giving without being replenished or without having some form of support that is healthy for you. Our bodies are not built to run as robots, although many people run their bodies as such. Our bodies have signals and gives us warnings and alerts when it has either had enough or when there is potential harm being done to it. The warnings can be the beginning signs of a shutdown, such as the following. You may begin to experience having chest pains, headaches, neck pains, shoulder pains, stomach problems, and the list goes on. These are some signs that you have reached a place of overload, or you are at a place of overload.

No one knows your how did I get here but you. If you were to be honest with yourself, you will come up with the answer. Food for thought, if you are not totally honest first with yourself, you will hinder your journey towards walking in a healthier and balance way of caring for others and even caring for yourself. No matter what your how is or was, address it so that you can rebuild and restore yourself back to a healthier and whole person. Remember this process is all about the caregiver not the person or people in whom you care for. Your how will awaken you to your why and your why will push you to your light of awakening towards balancing your own mental clarity.

Remember you are not giving up on your love one, you are just learning how to put yourself first so that you can be a better version and the best version of yourself. Don't beat yourself up for wanting to love on you again. Remember that your how is a reminder of how you got to the place you are at now. It's not meant for you to remain in an unhealthy place; but for you to grow and be replenished, rebuilt, and restored. Sometimes when life comes at us with a speed that is unfamiliar, we don't always have the right answers or tools on how to approach it or endure it in a healthy way. Look at this as an opportunity that you are taking to correct an issue that you didn't have all the right information to appropriately handle the task that was either placed before you or that you were thrown into. Either way, allow the how to serve as an awareness to make you a better you.

Space for your notes:

Write your answer here, how did you get here?

The Journey to Becoming a Healthier Whole You

Your caregiver journey starts with you, it is about you, and it is for you. I bet you thought I was going to say something really deep. Nope, this is where you take back your power and control. This is where you fix the broken, painful, overloaded, overburden and hurt places. For some of you, your pain took place over a period of time and for others, things just happened. Either way the process starts with you. Helping others can be hard especially if you are doing this with no formal training, support, or resources.

When I asked some caregivers, what did they do for self-care; many of them only gave me one part of their self-care practice, which was to go shopping, get their nails or feet done, buy a wig, get a massage, sometimes go with friends but not really, work longer hours, watch sports, or nothing at all. However, these things are good, but you still need to couple them with other things so that you are feeding your whole self. Which includes your mind, body, physical, emotional needs, along with your spiritual need. Learning and knowing what area that needs to be balanced and what areas that is out of alignment will teach you which area needs to be replenished.

Example:

Mind: Read, meditate, relax, watch a movie, do a word puzzle, spend time with positive people, watch YouTube videos that are positive, go get your hair done, do yard work, find a hobby, play chess, play board games, sew, go golfing.

Body: Walking, yoga, dance, tennis, riding a bike, swimming, walk the dog, massage, jogging, getting your feet and nails done, exercising, watching what you eat, keeping good hygiene, swimming, stretching your body daily.

Spirit: Practice breathing, read the bible or spiritual books or movies, spend time in nature, fasting, thinking positive, be still, be aware what you are feeding your mind and spirit, keep a journal, go on retreats.

Emotions: Balance and managing your emotions by having a self-awareness when your emotions are out of alignment, self-management of personal care, relationship management, social awareness, managing your stress, your mood, your anxiety, thinking through your options, respond don't react, knowing when you are overwhelmed and what to do, being emotionally aware of when you aren't getting enough sleep, realign your emotions by going on a weekend getaway or taking a long trip.

Physical: This could be you walking, stretching, taking kickboxing classes, hitting a pitching bag, making a diet plan for yourself, taking time to prepare healthy meals, going to the gym.

I would like for you to pay close attention to the different things that you can do that is listed under the varies areas. Of course, some of these things can be used interchangeably, but you get the drift. These things can be broken down further and you can add more to each. I won't go through the long list of things that you can do because I want you to sit down and think about the things that you can personally do for yourself. Also, ask yourself, how often are you providing healthy outlets for yourself in these areas? The list above is a very small list of things that you can do, and I am sure you can add more, which I am going to ask that you do. The journey to building a healthier whole you have to include you as well, as I stated before it's about you and it's about you practicing and applying a healthier method of care when it comes to you taking care of yourself. It's not only about one area but all areas. Sometimes we as people complicate taking care of ourselves. The other part is, for some of us we don't know how. Make the choice to start properly caring for yourself. Make time for you and manage your time appropriately so that you can also take better care of yourself.

Space for your notes:

What are you going to do in the following areas to take care of yourself?

Mentally:

_____
_____
_____

Emotionally:

_____
_____
_____

Physically:

_____
_____
_____

Spiritually:

_____
_____
_____

What do you currently do?

_____
_____

What area/s are you struggling in and why?

It's About Me Too

Caring for others is not only about the other person. It's also about you as well, meaning the CAREGIVER. This is the most important key factor that caregivers forget. Caregivers oftentimes make everything about the person or people in whom they are caring for. Nope, Nope, Nope!!! It is truly about you too. It's not only about what you do for others, but also how you care for yourself. When caring for others many caregivers take on the mindset that they have it all together and they don't need any help, they can handle it all by themselves until they can't. Most caregivers make things appear as though everything is good even when it's not or even when there not. Oftentimes caregivers take on the mindset that says, I will make it happen no matter what, even if I am hurting myself. Caregivers sometimes take on this mindset as well, nobody can do it the way it needs to be done or like I can do it. The list goes on and on of the many mistakes that caregivers make when it comes to not including themselves into the care plan.

As a caregiver, you have to get away from the mindset that; one you can fix everything or all things that your love one is dealing with or going through. Two, that you are the only one who knows best, or you don't need any help. Three, working without any support or resources, and not practicing self-care when and how you need to. You should also remember that you are only one person. I know that you would like to believe that you got this. However, what I would like to say to you is everyone needs someone in whom they can go to who understands their need and what they are going through. Someone who can understand when the caregiver needs help.

Once you learn that it's about you too, then and only then will you open up the door for you to begin to experience a new and healthier caregiving experience. Building and balancing your strength and support system will provide you with a better sense of mental clarity for yourself. Take time for yourself so that you can learn what you need for you. Learn when you need to fill your own cup. Learn before it's too late. You should never neglect yourself to care for other's because it is out of your fullness that others are able to get the care and love that you provide. It is also out of your strength, encouragement, empowerment, and willingness to do that your love one is able to receive the care that you are able to provide to them.

What are you going to do to add your own care into the care plan?

_____
_____
_____
_____
_____
_____
_____
_____

List why you matter

_____
_____
_____
_____
_____
_____
_____
_____

The Mask of the Caregiver

Most caregivers' handle wearing a mask well in the beginning until the mask begins to get to heavy to carry or it no longer hides the pain of the caregiver or the hurt of the caregiver and how overwhelmed the caregiver really is. The mask is an ugly lie and shield that is used to hide the many things that the caregiver doesn't want anyone else to see. If people were to see all that the mask covers then it will show how worn out, tired, frustrated, wounded, upset, lost, swamped, sleep deprived, overworked, confused, exhausted, and unbalanced the caregiver really is. As you can see the mask job is to cover up the caregivers need for help.

How do you remove the mask? Make the choice to put you first, know that you matter, learn to say no, balance all areas of your life, stop putting you last, stop making everyone issues or concerns a priority, surround yourself around people who can identify with what you are going through so that they can be of better assistance and support to you. Stop being shameful or prideful to acknowledge when you need help. Give yourself permission to love yourself, to like yourself, to be kind to yourself, to live life in balance and with a greater level of peace and joy. No one can remove your mask but you, with that being said, let today be the day that you remove your mask and never put it back on again.

Life can be a scary and difficult place when it feels like the weights of the world have been placed upon your shoulders. Nobody can get in the way of you becoming a better person, you just have to make the choice to become a better person who cares for yourself first; and one who doesn't wear a mask to cover up what you are going through. Don't be so concerned about when you take the mask off, what others might say. Focus on you and your own personal care.

Food for thought, what do you really have to lose at this point by taking the mask off. You will only continue to do more harm to yourself if you don't. Besides that, aren't you tired of living a lie and suffering in silence about what you cannot tell anyone or about what you are really going through. Aren't you tired of not living a healthy and balanced life? I dare you to take the mask off.

Name 5 things that hide behind your mask

_____
_____
_____
_____
_____

Write down how you are going to get rid of the mask

_____
_____
_____
_____
_____
_____
_____
_____
_____
_____
_____
_____
_____

Managing your Time

OMG, this is one of the biggest errors amongst caregivers. Many caregivers give every second and moment of their time, energy, thoughts and efforts to the person or people in whom they are caring for. Let's just imagine if you are the person who is giving all the things that I named and more, where is the time at for you? I'm not talking about when you squeeze yourself in or when you occasionally do something for yourself, but the time when you actually are managing your time on a daily basis where you are also caring for yourself. If you were to be honest this isn't happening as often as it should.

One of the wonderful gifts that a most women have would be the gift to nurture. Women more often than men go right into the gift to nurture when a need arises. This gift can be a blessing and a curse when not balanced. The reason why I say this is, anytime there isn't enough balance in what you do there will be a potential to become overwhelmed and sometimes feeling drained. Whenever there isn't enough balance oftentimes a person will experience burn out and fatigue.

Managing your time is about you staying balanced for yourself first. If you are great at caring for others but crappy at caring for yourself, ask yourself; who will eventually need care? Being a person who knows the importance of managing time contributes to you being and staying your healthiest and best person. I can't even begin to tell you how many people that I've met or either worked with who has become ill or who has experienced brain fog, mental fatigue, and physical tiredness from caring for others but forgetting to care for themselves in a healthy manner.

Most people aren't taught how to care for others and care for themselves at the same time. That's why managing your time is very important, because it teaches and shows you what you can do daily, how much you can do, what you can't do, and it also allows you to include yourself in caring for your own daily personal needs. Time is the one thing that we can't get back in life. Make the choice to make yourself just as important as the people or person that you care for. Don't let time get away from you and you look up and you ask the question as so many others do; how did I get here? How or when did I get to this place where I stop caring about me.

Space for your notes:

List why it is important to manage your time

_____
_____
_____
_____
_____
_____

List how you are going to better manage your time

_____
_____
_____
_____
_____
_____
_____
_____
_____
_____
_____

The Importance of Self-Care

I will start off by asking, what is self-care? Most people believe self-care is only about the things that a person does for him or herself. This is true to a degree, but it is more than just those physical things. Self-care is taking care of your well-being through restorative activities. Self-care is engaging and practicing what fills you up in every area of your life. Self-care is taking care of and balancing your mental, emotional, physical, and spiritual health. So often when you think about self-care it is mostly thought of from a physical act that is done for oneself, when self-care is so much more than that. Making you the priority should be the number one practice in self-care.

Self-care isn't how much you do for others as it is about taking care of yourself first. The major importance of self-care is taking care of YOURSELF first. You are only at your best when you are healthy in all areas of your life. Balance is what you practice and put into place, it's not what you think about doing but never do. Things can only change when you put forth the effort to do so. I am sure you can think of a hundred reasons of why caring for someone else is more important. I'm also certain that you can also think of a thousand reasons of why you believe that caring for others before your own needs are met is even more important, but the truth of the matter is self-care is the most important care we can give to ourselves and to others.

Mental health is here and the issues and concerns that surrounds mental health are here to stay as well. Caregivers must equip themselves with the proper information, education, support, and training to be better and healthier caregivers, first to self and second to others. The importance of caring for someone with mental health first starts with how we care for ourselves. The conditioning of the caregiver's role to care for others have been far under addressed and has come at a costly expense that may include the caregiver own physical or mental health. Caregiving is and can be a rewarding job as well as an exhausting job. As much as we would like to do everything and be all things to the people in whom we are caring for the reality is we can't, at least not without harming ourselves in the process. Remember to stay balanced, put yourself first by practicing healthy caregiving.

Name one new thing that you are going to practice for your own self-care in the area of mental, physical, emotion and spiritual care

_____
_____
_____
_____
_____
_____
_____
_____

List what you have learned about self-care

_____
_____
_____
_____
_____
_____
_____
_____
_____
_____

Communicating Your Needs

Why is it important for you to be able to express your needs. If you don't express your need or you don't know how to express your needs, then no one will know your need or know when you are at your ends or when you need a break from it all. The first thing that a caregiver must do is to realize that they have needs too. When communicating your needs, it is also important that you know how to express your need. You should always remember that your needs are just as important as the person or people in whom you are caring for.

Learning how to communicate your need is as simple as saying, I can't today. I won't be able to. I need time for me. I've scheduled time for myself today or for whatever day that is in question. I am taking a mental health or self-care day for myself. I'm tired, I'm exhausted, I feel like I need to regroup, I am not at my best right now. I need some time for me. Use words like I need, and I feel so that what you are communicating comes out clear so that others can understand what your needs are. When you don't effectively communicate your needs to others then they will not know what you need.

Also, you are not waiting for them to validate your need or give you there permission to take care of your needs. You are merely expressing your need so that they know why your need is just as important as their need. Remember you don't have to explain your why. You are giving notice of your own need without going into great details. Communication is your expression of your need not their permission to say yes to your need. Don't be so concerned about disappointing the person or people in whom you are caring for to the point that you are afraid to speak up for yourself. Communicate in love and not out of frustration. Don't lose sight when you communicate your needs, it's about you advocating for yourself. Care but don't hurt yourself in the process. Love but don't self-harm yourself. Speak to be heard rather you are misunderstood or not, you should communicate your need because this is your need.

Why should you communicate your needs

_____
_____
_____
_____
_____
_____
_____

*Why shouldn't you be afraid to advocate
for your own need*

_____
_____
_____
_____
_____
_____
_____
_____

Mental Clarity

What is mental clarity? Mental clarity is a state of mind in which you are more focused, and your perception is clearer. You are able to recognize, understand, and organize your thoughts. What are some causes for the lack of mental clarity? Overworking, lack of sleep, bad eating habits, not getting enough exercise, and being overly stressed. This is a short list of things but there are many reasons how people fall into a lack of mental clarity. How many times have you found yourself where you can't sleep, or sometimes not wanting to eat or overeating, or you weren't able to focus, or you forget things more often than you normally would? How many times have you found yourself where you have had frequent headaches, neck pain, or body aches? How many times have you found yourself where you felt like you are having an anxiety attack?

The lack of mental clarity has to do with the things that you deprive yourself of that you need balance in. Your mental clarity starts with you and ends with you. You shouldn't allow someone else mental disorder to change your mental clarity or your mental wellness. This is common for caregivers to do when caring for others. Food for thought, if you could save or take away the heavy burdens that your love one carries as it pertains to mental health, you would have already done so. You can only imagine what goes on inside of the mind of someone who has a mental illness. We don't know for sure what they truly deal with. Your mental clarity is what helps you to provide the necessary focus that is needed so that you can support your love one with the proper guidance and assistance that they need.

Nothing is more devastating then to wake up one day and realize that your own mental clarity is at risk. Balancing your mental clarity helps you to be fully present and engaged in the moment. Here are some things that you can do to improve your mental clarity. Plan your day the night before, be clear about where you are in your own mental clarity, have a healthy routine for yourself, unplug and step back, enjoy quiet time. Always stay focused on positive things. Remember that every crisis you won't have the answer and be ok with that. Practice keeping your mental health in a balanced and healthy state daily. You don't know what you don't know. However, when you learn better you should do better.

On a scale of 1-5 what number does your mental health fall in 5 being the best? What areas could use improving?

_____
_____
_____
_____
_____
_____
_____

What are 5 things that you are going to do to safeguard your own mental health

_____
_____
_____
_____
_____
_____
_____
_____
_____
_____
_____

Building a Support Team

Building or having a support team is about you and for you only. It is not for the person or people in which you are caring for. The importance of a support team is to give you the necessary support that you need when you need it. Ask yourself this question, how many people do you have who really understands what you are going through when you need to talk to someone, or when you need to vent without being judged. Who can you talk to that can identify or relate to what you are going through when caring for someone with a mental health illness? When you build a team or allow yourself to be surrounded around others who are going through or have gone through similar situations it gives you a small sense of relief that you are not alone. It gives you a place to express yourself without feeling pressured. Also, having a support team or attending a support group allows you to vent in a healthy environment without feeling like you have to explain your why or your how.

Oftentimes, when you are going through something and it looks different then what others can relate to, what you will find out is they sometimes don't know how to give you the support that you may need. Sometimes friends and family may not understand all that you are going through without saying what they wouldn't do or make comments like; I don't see how you take that, I couldn't. You want to be in a place where you feel safe to share your feelings and if you needed to cry you would be able to do so without being looked upon as though you were weak. A Support group or having a team allows you to have a healthy release of your tears, fears, and doubts without judgement. Sometimes just being around others who have gone through or are going through what you are experiencing will oftentimes give you the strength and support to continue your journey of caring for your love one with the reassurance and confidence that you may need. No one wants to feel like they are all alone. Unfortunately, some events in life may cause for you to feel like you are the only one going through what you are going through. But truthfully, you are not the only one, regardless of how you may be feeling. There are people who are going through what you may be going through, not in the exact way but with some of the same similarities. I encourage you to care about your well-being and mental wellness.

Who supports you when your mental health is being challenged?

Name three reasons why you should have a support system in place for yourself?

_____

_____

_____

Name three people that you are going to put into place for your support system.

_____

_____

_____

How often do you cry or how often do you hurt in silence?

_____

_____

_____

Are you in denial that you need support? Yes or No

Are you scared to go to a support group, Yes or No. If so, why?

_____

_____

Scheduling Time for Yourself

Is scheduling time for yourself the same as managing your time? No, it isn't. Managing your time is when you have already set a schedule and you are following what you have set for the most part. Scheduling time is when you actually take the time to put you into the schedule before it fills up. It's not about you squeezing yourself into the schedule. It's about you being a part of the schedule as you make it. The schedule shouldn't be one sided. It also shouldn't be about everyone but you. Making a schedule includes ALL parties meaning the caregiver. You have to balance what and how much you give because if you don't you will soon find your mental health being challenged. You will find yourself at a place where you have crashed and burned, meaning you aren't any good to or for yourself or no one else.

Too many caregivers give until they have nothing left. They give of themselves to the point where they are broken. Scheduling time for yourself is vitally importance for you as it is for the person or people in whom you are caring for. Knowing when you need care is even more important. When you schedule time for yourself, what you are saying is you are just as important as the person in which you are caring for. What it also says is that you care enough about yourself, and you are aware of your needs, and you recognize that your needs matter as well.

Mental health has been declared as an illness. It has many dark sides to it. Again, you can try to understand the pain of your love one; however, you will never really know their pain. Sometimes you will see their pain, or you may see them acting out or having a manic episode; but to understand what goes on in their mind you will never know. This is why scheduling time for yourself is about you and is important so that you can remain healthy.

Don't be afraid to spend time with yourself, care for yourself and to do things that build, replenish, and strengthen you. Don't live life secluded because of what you are going through with your love one. Stop suffering in silence because you think that no one understands you or you are too embarrassed to join a support group. Schedule time for you, arrange care for yourself.

Space for your notes:

Name three reasons why you are going to start scheduling time for yourself.

_____
_____
_____

Name three of your biggest concerns as to why you don't schedule time for yourself or enough time for yourself.

_____
_____
_____

Name three ways in how you care for yourself when you do schedule time for you.

_____
_____
_____

Name the people or person in whom you care for and why.

_____
_____
_____
_____
_____
_____
_____

Daily Affirmation

- ❖ I will provide support and assistance first to myself and not feel guilty.
- ❖ I will schedule time for myself to do the things that are needed for me.
- ❖ I will make sure that I am balanced in the following areas: Physical, Mental, Emotional and Spiritual.
- ❖ I will not allow the need of others to be more important than my own.
- ❖ I will make me a priority because I have learned that my needs are just as important as the people who depend on me.
- ❖ I will take the necessary time daily to regroup and restore my own mental clarity.
- ❖ I will no longer allow others to give me permission to take care of myself neither will I allow others to regulate my joy, pain level or happiness.
- ❖ I will initially love myself first while caring for the person or people who look for me to care for them.
- ❖ I will not live with any level of shame or regret about how I care for or how I am not able to care for my love one.
- ❖ I will live each day with hopes that my love one has better days then bad days. I will not allow their mental illness to affect my mental wellness.

- ❖ I will live in my today, and I will make a promise to myself to live one day at a time and to take one step at a time.

- ❖ I will not allow myself to be overwhelmed by the support or assistance that is needed to support my love one.

- ❖ I understand that mental health is an illness, and I can only do so much even though it hurts me to see my love one hurting.

- ❖ I understand that if I don't give myself a reset, or work on continual balance or maintain a level of peace; I too will become mentally fragile and depleted of my strength which will at some point place me in an unhealthy state.

- ❖ I don't have all the answers as to why my love one suffers with a mental illness; however, I will support and assist from a healthier place then what I previously have done.

- ❖ I am not neglecting my love one, I am learning a healthier way to care for them and myself at the same time.

- ❖ I promise to love them and love me at the same time. I promise to give care without hurting myself.

- ❖ I will make the choice to make caregiving a healthy experience for myself and for the person or people in whom I am caring for.

A Letter to my Future Self

www.ingramcontent.com/pod-product-compliance
Lightning Source LLC
Chambersburg PA
CBHW070441010526
44118CB00014B/2147